I0790526

Blessed and Cursed

True Encounter Stories

by

Jeffrey David Lilly Jr

As a kid growing up in Norwood Ohio, it was wild to say the least, being born an identical twin my life was going to be out of the ordinary. I just didn't know it yet. My identical twin brother Johnathan David Lilly, passed shortly after birth around 2:30am, and that crushed my father's soul. But in the last seconds before he lost his sanity, the doctor ran out into the hallway and yelled out "Mr. Lilly hurry back in because she's having another baby".

After my mom and dad got to hold me, they wanted to hold my brother Johnathan for a moment but he had disappeared. My mom was flipping out in the heat of the moment," where did you all take my baby to? "I want to hold him before you take him away to be cremated or whatever it is you do." They never brought him in, he was never seen again.

My mom always wondered what had happened to him. Maybe he was alive she said. They just never got closure on the situation with my brother and had no clue where he was buried. They felt like it itself was a cover up and that they had given Johnathan up for adoption without my parents knowing what had happened to him.

I was born shortly after at 2:36 and my dad settled down and I guess you could say I saved the day by being born into this world.

By the time I was 8 I could tell I was born with a set of gifts being an identical twin. I had already experienced Deja-Vu by that time a lot and I also had amazing skills as an athlete as well. I always took my sister Angie to and from school, it was my job, my mother said,being her older brother and all.

Life was about to change for me and get super serious from here on out. I'd experience some things most never get the chance to and I'd also get to see things that others would kill to see. Being an identical twin, in my opinion, would be a huge part of it all. The vibe I gave off, also many other factors, would come into play.

We always took Highland Avenue, it was at the top of Linden Avenue, where we lived. It was beautiful. Across the street were woods Indian Mound, an old Indian burial ground, sacred land. We knew all about the woods. They ran all the way up to North Woods at the top part of Norwood and over to Linder park and Paradise pond as well. There were railroad tracks that ran all the way through the middle of town.

On the way home from school one day my sister and I were a half a block away from home, when out of nowhere I hear a loud whoop and then a snort. Then a rock crashes right next to us 5 feet away. I quickly turn and look to see who was behind us and who threw the rock, but no one was there. The sidewalk behind us was empty all the way as far as I could see. I'm startled at this point thinking what just happened?

I turn to my sister and say well then let's go that was wild ,when all of a sudden, yet again, a loud whoop and a snort kind of like when a dog sneezes, and then again a bigger rock crashes closer this time to us. As it hits it shatters and we both jump off the ground to keep from getting hit. When we land, I turn quickly and scan the area, up in the woods was an opening with a couple small trees.

I see a creature bobbing its head left to right as it's shaking the trees moving evasively. This thing was huge. It stood 8 feet tall and was broad chested like a gorilla! But this was no gorilla. It had longer hair off of it's arms and legs, black and grey hairs layered perfectly from head to face to toe. Huge muscles, huge eye sockets. Its face was covered in hair except for the upper cheeks. A little bit of skin showed but it was a dark tan leathery color. Its nose was short from the bridge and rounded at the tip. Huge, immense, easily a good 600-800 pounds.

A coned head as well, flat out scariest looking thing I'd ever seen so far in my life. I turn to my sister and grab her hand and say run and don't look back. We make the turn to home, run down the hill and bust through the door yelling mom call the cops now there's a monster up in the woods. It was throwing rocks at us. My mom turns and says " you kids these days you're all crazy as hell" she says "now go to your room now and do your homework."

I remember that night being to scared to sleep. Afraid that if we did this creature would come through the window and take one of us if not both of us away and kill us. Needless to say after that incident we never went that route to school ever again. We took Harper avenue from that day forward.

I feel like this thing was lost looking for a way out of town. We were at the wrong place at the wrong time. Maybe it had traveled the railroad tracks at night and got stuck in the neck of the woods and we came through there and spooked it.

A few years later my best friend and I had decided to take a break from the local fishing hole we fished at, it had been fished out we felt so it was time to try to find a different spot. We were heading up to lake Cowan out in eastern Ohio. Chris said it was a good lake with plenty of Bass and Muskie. So I agreed it would be a good move to get to the lake right as it opened at 7 am.

We grabbed the first boat out and we were on the other side looking for the hotspot. We finally found a group of lily pads and we could see something banging the stalks on the cat tails below, they were moving like crazy. I tell Chris to throw anchor this is the spot and I start to tie on a silver spoon, a weedless one, perfect for the spot we were fishing.

I tell Chris to fish the front that I will fish the back, as I cast. I say don't hook me please brother as I start to reel my lure in I feel a jerk on my hat and it flys off into the water. What came next brought tears into my eyes as I felt my ear get ripped on and as I raised my hand up and put my fingers on my ear I felt warmth, and as I looked down at my hand it was totally covered in blood.

I realize I've been hooked in my ear. Chris looks over and says "oh man, Jeff I'm so sorry man I didn't mean to do that". I'm trying to pull the lure out of my ear but it's not working. I say take me to the bait house fast, I've got to get this out of my ear Chris. We get to the boathouse as the clerk comes out and says "what's wrong, supposed to hook the fish not each other fellas" and laughs.

Then the clerk says "I watched you hook him all the way from here. You all were directly across from the boathouse. So, I was ready" as he hands me a ruler and says "here bite on this" and pulls out a pair of metal snips. I bite down and hear a snap and the clerk slides out the lure and hands it to me. "Here ya go" he said. "Now put this on your ear" and hand me a bandaid.

I tell Chris let's go home this is starting to hurt. He says "oh really you don't Wanna try another place maybe Todds creek?" "There's good fishing there too, it's not far from here." I debate it for a minute then decide to go. About a thirty minute drive from where we were, we finally arrived at the farm. The area was all woods and soybean fields and corn fields and woods.

The walk to the hole in the fence line was about 600-700 yards, it felt like it took forever to get there, even with just a pole each in our hand. There was a huge white barn and a farmhouse behind us as we climbed through the fence hole. It was about 300 yards away. It was an old farmers land and Chris knew him so we had permission to fish there. We climb through the fence and wade out into the water and start casting.

We are catching one here and one there, Chris is 25 feet away below me. I'm up above by the waterfall. Todds Creek was an amazing place, the water was crystal clear. It was a Saturday, not even 8 clock yet, still early. I was thinking maybe the day will turn out okay after, all when out of nowhere a rock came crashing into the water next to me.

I thought okay where the hell did that just come from what could of thrown that, I look down towards Chris, he's fishing, working on bringing in a white bass he'd hooked, so I didn't have to bother to ask if he threw the rock. I knew better, but just to let it out. I say Chris brother you just throw a rock at me? he said "now you just seen me bring a bass in so, you know better."

I reply, well something just did man and it does not make sense what does that? I said to him. He looks at me astonished, "like really for real, wow." I said yes and it was a good sized rock I said, but I quickly brushed it off. But I'm thinking deeply now ,wow what was that shit,what was that?

15 minutes later, out of nowhere, as I'm casting another rock comes in from the side of the woods as before, the opposite side from where we came in, nothing but deep deep woods. As it hits next to me, by a foot, I look down to Chris as he's looking at me already, our eyes meet and off we run through the water trying to get out of the creek as fast as the water will allow.

We're both scared to death at this point trying to climb up the water drenched bank . As we are climbing up out of the water, we're slipping and sliding but slowly getting out. We get to the fence and climb through the hole and trying to run down the fence line. My legs are like rubber. I'm so afraid something's gonna come out of the woods and grab one of us. The whole situation was not normal.

Chris looks over at me and says "what the hell was that?" "Not once but twice, threw rocks at you in the creek, there is not a soul out here Jeff" he says. "We're out in the middle of nowhere, it's 8 am on a Saturday, what was that" he repeated. I say, I don't know but something about this whole day is off. Were almost to the truck about a 100 yards away when we heard a pack of wild dogs chasing something through the woods. "Now what is that?" Chris says.

Probably whatever was throwing rocks at me had it's scent picked up by those dogs, I say. "But a raccoon doesn't throw rocks! There are no bears out here, so what in the hell is going on" Chris says again! We finally get to the truck and throw the poles in the back of the truck bed. Chris has the keys but can't get them in the ignition. They fly onto the seat and I grab them and put the key in and turn the truck over and automatically roll the window down.

I tell Chris go as he stomps the pedal to the metal and we peel off out of there,never to return. We never fish Todds creek ever again. After that it was back to route 32 to fish but we'd started to hear stories while down there as well about a wild man running about in the woods chasing campers off. We fished the slab on the right side of the river, everyone else fished the left side that was thick woods. There were woods on our side too, just more opened up and less thick.

Even a group of our older friends fished the left side opposite side of us. They were even talking about this wild man they said that he looks like a man that just got dropped off one day in the woods and was left there forever. He had hair all over his body,head to toe they said. He was crashing through campsites and destroying people's gear and tents ,as well as yelling loud weird sounds and making weird, odd noises.

So, we never fished that side but we stayed alert while down there fishing at night or on the slab. Some nights our hair would stand on end as we were down there. The hair on our arms and our necks as well as our heads even. Seemed like we were being watched the whole time. We kept the fire going higher than usual to keep whatever it was that may have been out there, away from us as much as possible.

Eventually we stopped fishing there. It was all changed, later, into a park and a bike trail. It was a few more years down the road, I had not fished as much. I started a family and worked two jobs to keep them up. I would fish the weekends mostly. On a late September day my uncle Mike came to the house to ask if we wanted to go to his buddy Toms to Bass and Crappie fish the night. Now we'd been up there but only at daytime, this would be life changing, I just didn't know it yet.

It was a hour drive out to Toms, he lived next to the Miami Whitewater forest and park, he had land next to it. A beautiful place. We get there and get out. We grab our gear and start to make the climb. It started out flat but angled up as you went up to the right. It sloped down to the river and on the right was a ridge that wrapped around to lake two. The ridge was high as the eyes could see. Thick woods on the left all the way up to the top, then it leveled out.

Up close to the top, the climb became a 90 degree angle up the middle. By the time we got to the top we were winded. You had to set your gear down and bend over to catch your breath. On the north side there was another climb up to lake two, it was a 200 yard climb from there. At lake one you sat in kind of a half bowl type setting. The left side was all thick woods straight up to lake two. The woods went all the way to the water damn well near in the left side, about 3 feet from the water. It was hard to fish the left side.

The cows were over on the left at the front of the lake,in the shade, laying down relaxing. Half were drinking from the lake. We were all using artificial baits catching bass left and right and good ones too. It was always worth the climb up there, even for late September it was a warm day, but not too hot. The day went so fast it seemed but it always did while we were up there, as they say time flies when you're having fun.

The sun started to set, my dad and my uncle's were spread out, everyone was settling into their own spot for the night part of this trip. This is when we got super serious, we took account of what each one had caught throughout the day and kept track of who was in 1st, 2nd, and 3rd, thats how competitive we were at everything we did. We had it down to a science it seemed.

At nightfall it got very quiet. All of a sudden the fish stopped biting and at about 12 midnight the cows got up and walked off to the right side and went up the hill towards lake two, instead of going right and down the slope to the river. Which seemed odd but like I said we'd never been up there at night, so maybe that's what the cows did. I shrug off the thought of them leaving and kept on fishing.

About an hour later we hear something way up on the ridge coming down slowly. The crackling of the leaves on the forest floor, the twigs and branches snapping and popping as well, loudly. We thought it was deer by the sounds we were hearing and just kept on fishing. Whatever was up there though kept moving more evasive and more methodical. The closer it got towards us,about an hour later, we weren't hearing the sounds anymore but the fishing totally shut down all the way.

I knew where a spot was on the left that was five feet deep! I was debating a move over there and was already tying on my next setup. I had a slip bobber and a crappie hook setup for 3 feet deep. I grabbed the lantern and my pole and started to make the move over.

As I made the turn, I saw something crouching down on two legs but this thing had it's right arm down in the lake and had it's hand cupped trying to get a drink of water. It had fur perfectly layered from head to toe. It's back was towards me but was at an angle. I held out the lantern, it was on this thing perfectly. I could see it's whole body. It finally realized it had been spotted.

 It slowly pulled it's huge hand out of the water. I could see water dripping off it's huge hand back into the lake slowly, as it turned towards me, as well as it's head over it's left shoulder. I could see it's mouth slowly opening as it turned my way. It's eyes were glowing a yellow with the light on it. I could also see it's teeth. Four canine teeth, not sharp but worn down and kind of rounded and square teeth as well. A full mouth of teeth. It had a baby doe held down with its left hand. The baby deer had no chance to get away.

Its muscles were solid looking, impressive. It was about four feet wide while crouched and about 500 pounds. It let out a snort at the end kinda sounded to me like a dog sneezing, as if this thing were disgusted that it had been seen. At this point I'm froze in fear, face to face with this wicked yet beautifully laid out creature I'd had an earlier encounter with as a kid. We were at a standstill now, it was frozen too, almost like a spooked deer in headlights.

Glancing at me while crouched down then glancing at the woods as if it wanted to run but couldn't. At that moment I hear my dad and my uncle's whispering, "jr what is that you see?" "What is it?" I'm slowly coming back to reality when I hear them saying it over and over. I take one more look at this creature, totally in shock. The makeup of this thing was wild built to survive.

I turn at this moment and yell out "go now run down the mountain now!!" I bolt, dropping my pole but holding on to the lantern so I could see. They go jumping over the side of the hill and hit the slope running. I'm right behind them. I make my jump and soon I'm out in front of them. I'm slowly raising the lantern up so we could all see where to go. As I do, I slowed down ever so slightly only to be taken out from the backside by my family from behind.

We all go tumbling end over end down the mountain. End over end, I'm trying to gain control of my legs so I can get up and run. But I can't. My legs are like rubber bands, I can't get them out from under me. I'm rolling into logs and and over rocks trying to push off of them and get up but couldn't. It felt like forever getting to the bottom of that mountain. Finally getting to the parking lot at Toms house, we stop all in a circle, we're all bent over sucking air to catch our breath.

What was that jr there all saying, as I say shut up you know damn well what we saw why do you gotta ask me for. We all seen the same damn thing. Tom comes out at this time and says "what's all the ruckus I heard y'all coming down the mountain in a hurry?" My uncle Mike walking over slowly towards Tom he says "awe we just got spooked by something up there". That's all my uncle mike said.

"I figured as much" Tom says, "I've been finding dead animals up there a lot lately". "A couple rabbits, even a deer off the slope" he says. "Glad none of my cows aren't missing!" My uncle Mike says "well they rolled out, they are up by lake two, at least they were when we left."
"That's wild" Tom says, " they never go up there! They always go down by the river." "I will go check on them tomorrow, Tom says, and walks back in his house, " goodnight fellas good seeing yas again."

 We all are grouped into a circle and Mike says listen "we can't be telling any of what we just witnessed up there on that mountain, we have to make a pact to keep this a secret." "If people find out they will be up there hunting them things and it'll piss Tom off and we won't be allowed to fish here ever again." We all agreed on it as we were each getting in the car. What was funny was we never went back after that.

Uncle Mike went back to get our gear the next morning but armed with a pistol of course. After that night it all came together for me slowly. I knew now what it was that I had experienced in life not one but three different encounters with these things. So many others have not been blessed to even see or have one encounter. All of the stories, all of the tips about being in the woods and what to look for, what to pay attention to as well, that to all who went out the door that night. My life was definitely changed after that I struggled with alcoholism and drug addiction, jail and prison as well was in that mixture.

It was in these times that I could sit back clear my mind and reflect on not just the 3 main encounters that had happened but all of them and how they were all tied in together to one another. Life gives us all a path it's how we choose to go through and handle each situation that forms us for who we are to become later in life. Successful or to become a failure and I sure didn't wanna go out of this world known as a failure. I just couldn't break free of this curse I was stuck in at this point in time.

I'd taken a downward spiral after all of the things. I'd become a witness, they become true, real to me, only to have made me a complete basket case. I'd promised to keep it a secret because of what others might say or do. I didn't want people up on Tom's land hunting that creature I'd seen or bothering him in any way. It wasn't until my fiance became sick with a life threatening disease.

I would sit down think it over and later decide to do a tell all about what I had seen out there in the woods. I did an interview with my friend from sasquatch theory and after that it just took off. Buckeye bigfoot and Cryptids Canada, took encounter reports and made personal videos of my encounters and put them on youtube. Last but not least my buddy Vic Cundiff attempted to do a live video with me about my encounters he said to me Jeff! push for the truth, get it out there.

And to work with others in any way and every way you can. And it felt so good to just get it off of my chest. It is no longer buried from deep within me. It had taken off and I felt so relieved now at this point. And I'm able to concentrate on life now especially being in recovery now away from all the bad chemicals that destroy one's soul. Let me tell you the old myth that once you see one of these creatures they say your cursed your life and soul are tested.

I feel it was worse on me because I kept it a secret and it slowly engulfed me as a person as a human being and my soul was disturbed from deep within me. To have seen something not many others ever have the chance to see is one thing but to keep it in the dark from the world puts this on a whole other different level. All of the experiences that I was having, its exactly how it felt to me having went through all of the things I went through spending so many years in the woods.

I was enjoying myself so much, feeling so free and so many times, I realize now, I wasn't even paying attention to my situations because of the happiness and joy the woods brought me, while fishing and camping. I probably wasn't even paying attention over half the time I was in the woods to my surroundings. Now honestly how scary is that? Like I was saying so many things are unknown out there in our oceans and forests still not proven yet to this day.

So many sightings and incidents and reports have gone unnoticed, not counting the missing 411 reports totally different subject. Safety in the woods is not practiced as it should be these days. Like my uncle Jack had always said to me if you're ever in the woods and all of a sudden you feel like your being watched or your hair stands up on the back of your neck or arms go get out of the area, put your head down and just go.

My uncle Jack Vilvens had seen so many things out there in the woods he spent ¾ of his life in the woods. An old Arkansas Razorback, his daddy used to give him one bullet while living as a young man in Pine-Bluff Arkansas and tell him go get dinner, you miss we are starving tonight his dad would say. He became a good shot at a very young age.

He said he'd had feelings of being stalked while he hunted sometimes, even felt being the hunted sometimes while hunting he said. And it didn't happen all the time he said, but it happened enough times for him to realize he wasn't the only one out there in those woods. He said there was something out there with me almost mimicking my moves, it felt like sometimes he said. And it happened to him even when he moved to West Virginia. It totally freaked him out he said.

But that's when he met my father Jeff Lilly Sr. and Mike Lilly and Rocky Lilly my two uncle's and also there sister Brenda Lilly, which became his wife shortly after.,They had all told me of encounters they'd had while hunting in the mountains of Beckley West Virginia. The feelings of being stalked while on hunts down at Beaver Creek. They had experienced a bunch of wild howls at night but they were not wolves. They said, the sound was so powerful it felt like it tore right through them as if it were letting every living thing out there know these are my woods.

Something that loud could not be human. To be able to make sounds that loud to be able to travel as far as they did, had to have a huge lung capacity. It totally spooked them. Some nights they would pack up and just leave. Thats the difference maker in it, all hunters pay attention to detail, tracks, sounds, weather wind etc. Fisherman are nine out of ten times gonna be paying attention to the water not the land.

Compared to hunters they notice everything. They warned me the first time I ever went fishing.

Rule 1 - was no horseplay ever. It causes accidents that could end up deadly.
Rule 2 - pay attention to details in your surroundings.
Rule 3 - never walk into a water source without company and always take something to check the depth of the water your going into.
Rule 4 - was if you get lost stay still don't move someone will find you, never go any further once you're lost.

These were rules coming from my family even though they didn't think I payed attention I always was. I looked up to them. My uncle Jack was a professional Bass fisherman and my uncle Mike was an ex Army Ranger with two tours in Vietnam. They knew there stuff and they taught me so much. I felt like what they taught me helped me in each encounter that I experienced.

It was crazy to even fathom that my life would unravel the way that it did. Not one but three encounters with sasquatch or bigfoot by the age of 25. There are many names for these creatures but,there is also a huge indifference between believers and non believers as well. I was a non believer at an early age. I found out very soon in life what was really living out there in the woods across the world.

Having an encounter at 8 years of age and then yet another at 16 and then a full on closeup with a sasquatch at the age of 23. It was all kind of like a visual crossword puzzle for my memory to be able to handle each piece that was slowly being worked into place until it was finished. But it was slowly affecting me mentally. Slowly but surely building me up for the next one, it seemed as each one took place.

But it was at this time my soul had been really affected by what I had seen in my life. I started drinking. Then I started drinking more and more, eventually I was up to a case of beer per day at the bar by myself. Then came the cocaine in the mix. It'd be a case of beer and $25.00 worth of cocaine to a case and $200.00 worth a week. I was working to stay numb. My health started to get horrible. My teeth started to go bad as well.

Now the picture was becoming so much more clear. Yes I had been put through too much for my mind to handle. I was a shell that was slowly cracking. I had seen so much but what I was seeing was very touchy to even try to communicate about it to others. I couldn't even do that. Then having been put in a pact with my family to keep my mouth shut,that was a very bad choice I had made.

When you see something of that significance you don't suppress it. That is dangerous. I'd end up seeing a psychiatrist but it was not for what I had seen,it was for what I was doing to myself after the fact was put right before my face. I ended up being diagnosed with Social Anxiety disorder and Agoraphobic. Something had traumatized me but I couldn't say what it was out of fear of being labeled crazy or put out in the nuthouse.

At 27 years old inquiry my job as a plant manager of a paper recycling company, Recycling Express and as a shipping and receiving manager at another paper recycling center, Omaha

Paperstock. I was in a bad bad place. I was really suffering from something horrible and it ended up keeping me in the house for a year. And If I didn't leave when I did I would come straight back home or end up at the Emergency room of a hospital.

They would say we don't know what the problem is, its odd but there is nothing wrong with you. We can find anything. But something was clearly off big-time. Out of nowhere I would get sick to my stomach and start sweating and my heart would race. I would think heart attack and tell my girlfriend this is it, this is the big one, call an ambulance I'm dying. Time and time again it would happen until I was shut in behind closed doors a prisoner of my own home.

What had happened was I had been so traumatized and my mind couldn't take in what it had seen. I was in a battle with my conscience and I was losing fast it seemed. I was a lost soul. I didn't know what was happening, thought at times maybe I was going crazy. But didn't know why. I had several incidents with the unknown or American folklore and couldn't understand why it was happening to me over and over again not once but 3 weird experiences.

It was at this time I only knew of one thing left to do and that was just start over. Start fresh try to figure out how to beat these overwhelming feelings I was having. But how was the question? So I started practicing meditation. So when it happened, I could end it quickly. The breathing control really helps me as well. Slowing things down and controlling the situation upon me.

It took time but within 6 months of changing things my life became manageable for a while, but not for long. I woke one day and my face was swollen so bad I couldn't get out of bed. The ambulance was called. I was rushed to University Hospital in Cincinnati and admitted. They thought it was an abscessed tooth that needed attention. They prescribed me some pain killers called Vicodin and some antibiotics Penicillin VK and made me an appointment for a dentist in behind the hospital.

U.C Dental Department Oral Surgery, my next stop. It too would be a bad deal for me. The problems with my teeth kept coming and going. They would say it was a bad tooth and pull it.
But it just kept happening over and over. Finally, what happened was they finally realized after it was too late to fix,that there was a bigger problem. What had happened was my teeth had been all separated from their roots.

An old baseball injury had really hurt my teeth. When I was warming up a pitcher one day before a game I had not put on my catchers helmet,it was a hot hot August summer day so I kept it off to stay cool. As I was warming up a pitcher, who threw a fastball clocked at 85-87 mph, I had suddenly blacked out from the heat as he threw the ball and hit me directly in the mouth.

It was at that moment it made impact so hard it separated my roots from my teeth so perfectly when they snapped on contact. The roots laid back down in place and it wasn't showing up on a dental X-ray. That would end up costing me all of my teeth. I threatened lawsuits and was in so much pain, In the end, I would have two masses growing in behind my nose from this happening.

Getting the call from a Dr. to come in and have a sit down. Possibly the news of the big C word coming my way. Cancer, I would have to have a biopsy which ended up being good news finally for once, but surgery was still needed to remove the tumors. The damage was done at this point. No teeth left in my mouth and a whole in my upper gum that never fully closed after being stitched. The infection had ate some of the bone away.

I'd be promised to be totally fixed by my dentists, who had

dropped the ball on me,and couldn't figure out my case. They felt bad for not being able to figure the problem out for several years. I'd say four years,but I was never fixed and they were just trying to cover their own asses on the error they'd made. I eventually got used to how I looked and eventually it didn't affect my pride at all. It wasn't my fault.

But I clearly started to feel like I was cursed, how could I not. To much had happened to fast for it to be a coincidence. I started really trying to figure out what was going on. There were several things that were off at that time. I was in a horrible relationship but the talk that came about my way one day startled me. My father had been having an affair with one of my good friend's mother and they had been caught. The rumor was the woman my dad had been seeing studied black magic.

Now that made a little sense to me but was scary and seemed a little far fetched. I knew who Sylvia England was. I grew up in her home throughout the years. Hell, they lived right below us. The talk was that she had put a spell on my family because my dad had ended their relationship and she was heartbroken over him. So she had placed a spell on us. That was the rumor and it went in and on and grew from there.

My dad would soon clean the slate with my mom and Sylvia and eventually after dad had his first stroke, they would become friends again, shortly after. My mom was something else. She had a heart of gold. She would help others anyway she could,people would be laying across our floor when my dad would get off work from General Motors at night second shift. Dad would get in a little after 11 when he did come home, not often but when he did, this would be his reason for running the roads later he said.

It was at this time I was healing up from having the tumors removed but in pain from being cut open. I started to abuse the Percocet that was now being prescribed to me by my surgeon. I was becoming an addict at this time, I had to keep a whole bottle of painkillers. If I got half empty I was calling for a refill. And my Dr's became upset with me for calling. Hell I'd even called my surgeon's house on Christmas day because I was gonna be out by the end of that night.

That's how bad it got and fast addiction was no joke and I was about to find out. But this was just the beginning, the Nightmare was later to come. I would later get into an altercation with my girlfriend at our house and was stabbed in my arm with a butcher knife. An artery was hit but I had no clue. I was high on seroquel one day and decided I was going to confront her about an affair I thought she was having.

I came home from work one evening and started to argue. Quickly it escalated and I was stabbed several times with a butcher knife, shed hit an artery. I was bleeding like a gutted pig all over the living room floor. I grabbed a towel and wrapped my arm and called my aunt Wendy, who picked me up and drove me to Jewish Of Kenwood Hospital. In the Emergency room I told them it was an accident, the doctor knew better. He told me to tell the truth or suffer with pain. He said I will give you something good if you tell me who did this.

If not you will suffer and boy did I suffer and badly. I wouldn't tell who'd done this to me so I was given tramadol a pain killer but not for no stabbing was it going to cover the pain. I would suffer many sleepless nights in pain and crying like a baby. I remember it like it was it was yesterday. My whole paycheck that week I bought painkillers with it. I couldn't take that pain it was so intense, being stabbed was no joke, I now knew the pain of that as well.

After 4 weeks I was back to normal no pain from my earlier injury. I was now super hooked to pain pills, didn't matter as long as I was high. I shot up the ladder very fast and within a couple years I was using every drug known to man to numb my life's pain. From percocet 30mg to Morphine 30mg,60mg, time released beads. I would crush those and snort them Oxycontin 20mg, 40mg. Same pattern. I was getting bad. I was working for a local freeman named Kenny Helms Sr.,a good friend of my father's, he hired me after dad had his stroke and was put into bed for good.

We would start our day at the shop crushing and doing pain pills before the equipment even got touched, then we would go do the job on the schedule. Get paid and then go on the hunt for the next days meds if we were out. What a life I was living, I thought I was doing good. That is denial 101 at its best working on one's self. Kenny would later be diagnosed with liver cancer and would pass 6 months later, God bless his soul he worked hard.

He was the best freeman I'd ever seen, he would get in a 100 pine tree, rope in spur up to the top in less than 8 minutes and be cutting. I enjoyed working with him and he always paid me very well but I worked hard for my money as well. I'd introduce Kenny to my buddy Johnny B Goode,was his nickname. Johnny had it all, a walking pharmacy at his house. Johnny made our lives easier everyday. It was only when Johnny was out gambling at the casinos we'd be in trouble sometimes lay sick for a couple days until Johnny came home.

After we laid Kenny to rest, I stopped working for good. I had gone through so much pain and hurt from being injured to watching others around me die from disease or most of the time an overdose, there for a 20 year stretch I would wake up daily looking on Facebook to see which if any friends or family had passed from overdose the night before. Life was insane for me at this time. I was a walking time bomb waiting to explode.

I would struggle for a total of 12 years with abuse of substances after alcohol. It seemed to be overlapping and consuming my life. I was in a battle for survival 24/7 and at anytime I could lose the fight. I had my whole family against me. I was homeless and out in the streets doing whatever it took to stay numb. It got to the point where my family fully shut me out of their lives and I finally came out of denial and seen I had a huge problem.

I did wake up and eventually check myself into the Salvation Army alcohol and drug addiction program. I did manage to stay sober for 6 months and left one day before graduation. A close friend had passed from staph infection from drug abuse and I wasn't missing his funeral. He had daughters by my sister. She was hurting deeply and this was when I really made the promise to stay sober. My family allowed me home and I was kind of happy again. But I still had things hidden suppressed secrets that had to come out.

It wasn't going to get all the way better for me until this happened. I just didn't see that being the problem. I soon placed myself into a medication based treatment program and I was doing good things again. Staying sober, and helping others. I was sick of losing all of my close friends to this disease. I was dead set on making a difference in this world and I did do so. I devoted myself a little bit too early and messed up a couple times but soon I was whipping addiction. I finally completing a goal.

I was making so much of an impact on others that they were totally committed to push themselves to get sober too. And I loved that this was happening. I had seen so much bad I was praying God would allow for me to see some good for once, not that I deserved it, but I had put in a lot of hard work in the process of it all. And it was starting to pay off. I just at some point had to come all the way clean about the secrets I was keeping locked inside or I was going to spiral again and I didn't have another one left in me.

So I sat down and weighed my options out. I would write my full life and tell all in a nutshell of moments I was traumatized by the most. Hell it would be enough they were all oh so true. People go through some stuff but, not like this.

Starting off the bat, I would lose my brother then I would lose my uncle Lester sheldon, first full blown alcoholic 20 years, turned good, found God became a brother of a church. Only to love and talk about the Lord so much not one person would give him a job. He ended up taking his own life within a months time of being saved and baptized.

It crushed all of us badly inside. I stopped going to church for a long time. After that, we all did then shortly after losing Lester. We lost my uncle Chris to Leukemia that was difficult as well. Then my aunt Brenda went a few years after her brother, these were my dad's siblings, my aunts and uncles. Next we lost uncle Buhl right after that, then papaw passed on good Friday that was really tough on me.

It felt like we were cursed at this time. My father was having an affair and the woman was supposed to be studying and reading black magic, a very dangerous practice. We were all having bad luck, my whole family even our friends too.

Everyone around us was having horrible luck, hell even our friends were too, having bad luck. It was a crazy time. Only after mom and Sylvia, my dad's mistress, became friends again did the bad luck begin to subside slowly.

A very wild time in my life so many kisses, not counting what had already happened, plus encounters with unworldly creatures and incidents one after another. It was easy to see something was off about the whole situation. I had no clue what to do to fix it consumed by drugs, alcohol, no where to turn. Then pow, dad has a major stroke, bed ridden from there on out. Then mom has a stroke but mild then a heart attack after that.

She heals up finally then we lose my grandma Hazel. She coughed and busted her Aortic valve in her heart. What kind of luck is that. It just didn't make sense, not any of it. I was mad as hell at this point.
Decided to get straight, fight for my life, not give up for my sake and my kids' sale as well. Then my brother goes to prison, comes home then my youngest son Luke goes. He comes home then a year later, my little brother dies out of nowhere.

Fought me so hard to get sober only to hide his addiction and that really got me good there. Now I am getting ready to consult a psychiatrist about having possible PTSD. What was weird was I dreamed of a bible being suspended in the air in my bathroom and I would get up to go get it and as soon as I went to grab for it the Bible lights up a star pentagram right around where it says holy bible. Two weeks after that dream we'd lose my brother at 4 am. With all of us just across the street from him.

Just too many things that were all bad in my life outweighed the good. Its almost as if it weren't for seeing the unknown, there wouldn't have been anything worthy, except my helping others living for god. Help pulling people from the fire of addiction and helping out when they needed an ear and giving the best advice I could. They had no clue I was just as bad off if not worse.

For the non-believers. you need to get out in the woods more. Maybe you will have an experience. For those of us who have had an encounter or a sighting we already know what's out there so there is no need. We have been there and done that, so having done my research over the years has taught me quite a lot about these wicked yet beautiful creatures,animals,hybrid hominids etc. So many opinions out there.

There has been an estimate given as of year 2020 by bigfoot experts on the total population of these things it sits at 4,000 range more or less ,it's just an estimate. Sasquatch are known to migrate but no one has a clue any pattern that exists. There still hasn't been any bones from a skeleton found as of yet, no scientific proof exists that really proves there existence. Other than hair samples and many tracks that have been cast. As well as videos and sighting reports.

Only those of us who have had a full on sighting as myself, know the full truth that's why I decided to write my tell all about sasquatch and all I've learned. To also have huge pieces of the puzzle to contribute to push the truth out there with my colleagues. We're so close yet so far away from the proof we need to prove they exist. The researching goes on 24 hours a day 7 days a week. We have found out they live off the land. The natural resources mother earth has provided for them.

They have adapted to all known areas they live in. They are known to hunt deer and elk and moose, even fish. They are believed to be a very powerful specimen and can travel very fast over huge amounts of land. Arms and legs and feet as well as a mid-tarsal break at the ¾ mark of the foot. Known to be able to twist branches like they are nothing. And to pull small trees from the ground and shove them back in upside down, that takes raw power to be able to do the things they do.

I don't say why because I have seen 2 in my years on this earth and have had several other incidents as well. I have to say life was a real challenge for me after they happened. I struggled with alcohol for 10 years. I became a full blown alcoholic trying to suppress what I had seen and keep my feelings locked deep down inside me. After putting alcohol down because of the damage it was doing to my body,only to pick up yet another addiction.

I became overwhelmed again only to become addicted to pain killers. I would take anything that would kill the pain. All the way up the ladder to becoming a heroin addict for 10 years,knocking on death's door daily for years. I finally woke up to what reality really was for me on December 23, 2014 and decided to get sober to deal with every problem I was having in life and battle it head on. I have been in recovery for 6 years now.

I help others when the chance presents itself. When covid hit in 2020 we were all put into a different mind frame being forced mentally to think on the defensive mode a lot. Many more challenges arose for my fiance and myself in March of 2021 were hit with the fact that she has a rare disease called RB-ILD and she has 3-5 years to live, I was confronted with my inner being. I started to be self conscious of what life was really about.

This would be the reason for me letting it all out, putting all my cards on the table regardless of who said what! I was putting it out there and I'd work with whoever possible to do my part and help put my pieces of the puzzle together. I reached out later to who would become a friend of mine over at Sasquatch theory. Brian and I did my first interview and I was off and running.

It went so well I decided to go further with it. I lined up a few more interviews for youtube channels who wanted to put my story out there,and it blew up way faster than I thought it would. The Vic Cundiff interview for his show on Dogman encounters, really started the uproar of shows wanting to do interviews with me about my story. And I went from the bottom all the way to the top of the ladder. I had done a couple bigfoot shows on youtube, as well as many videos.

But there were some areas I was lacking knowledge wise when It came to these beautiful creatures. I ran across a person that would befriend me and teach me so much more. His name was (Albert Edsma),a native Indian from California. It was at that time I was made aware of my situation. These creatures are drawn to certain people. Ones with pure souls, givers not takers in life, they are so intuitive they can pick out people that are special kind of people. And they will follow you while in the woods and they will let you know they are there. They will lightly interact and let you know they are there.

But also if you try to get a good view or picture or video they will toy with you as they already know what your planning. They will mimic your every move and totally take you out of your element of surprise. Sasquatch are very intelligent that's how they've made it this long out in our forests across the world. They are very defensive and evasive creature and move methodically.

Why they are so hard to pinpoint is this reason as well. They are so keen on the subjects that they are studying. Every move they make is defensively as well as offensively to stay safe and out of site. On the west coast, California,Washington,and Oregon, the forest helps keep them covered so we'll. But in late August they take up and migrate down from the higher elevations before the snow pack comes in and forms.

They follow all the other animals that are migrating as well, to keep their food source in abundance. As they migrate down into the valleys away from the snow to the lower elevations they meet up with other clans. Its here the western clans and the eastern clan exchange mates before moving on into the Joshua's creek area following the herds of animals to sustain themselves.

The will even go as far as to go into the rivers and grab beaver and feed off of them as well.

They will feed off of deer and elk, and burrough, as well as wild hog who migrate there as well. Until the snowpack melts and they make their climb back up into the 9,000 ft. mark of the Sierra, and Shasta mountains. And it's believed they mate up there in the spring. People believe the game trails in these areas were made by the animals,they were really formed by the sasquatch traveling them and migrating in them day and night.

It is thought to be that these creatures are mean but they are mostly not. The sasquatch that live in the national parks where there is thick forest for them to stay hidden are more laid-back and kind. The ones who reside as loners or small clans are the ones to watch out for, they have less forest to protect them. So they have less food and game to sustain them, these are the ones that will steal fish from fisherman and scare hunters away from a kill to take their food.

It is known that they learn quickly and act efficiently to survive. Stories from the 1970s were reported that the trout that were being stocked in the lakes and streams abundantly. Sasquatch learned this movement and acted on it. As the drivers would pull out after a stocking the sasquatch would move and pull out huge amounts of fish to the point stocking had to be stopped.

As well as drivers quitting their jobs at a rapid pace from having sightings and encounters with them over this issue. It was to hard to keep drivers that would haul the fish in out of pure fear of these creatures, once the stories started to pour out of that area. So the project ended then completely. It was soon after that stories of missing kids were starting to come out. Then one day in 1973 a young girl went missing while camping. Search teams had gathered shortly after and local police as well.

The search went on for two days and two nights before finally it came to a happy end and the girl had been found over 45 miles away, over 2 separate mountain ridges away. A driver coming through the roads of the mammoth mountains was driving along and reported to have seen a huge arm come out of the woods only to sit this girl out on the edge of the road. Safely returned with only her pants on. She made it out alive but it could never be proven what it was that returned her.

The senior rangers had always known they'd existed they would encounter them regularly. But just kept it to themselves. Every once in a while campers could be seen flying out of a camping site leaving all their gear behind and a couple days later other campers would see the local rangers go into the campsite and gather up all of the gear that was left behind by others who had seen something and fled the site so quickly.

Even in Ohio,a story came out about a young girl who had lived with her grandparents. They had encounters with several sasquatch. Later when her grandparents passed away she kept the farm and the land and had made friends with a bigfoot who would come and try to get sugar from her. One day her friend said why don't you get a hair from him and tell him you will give him sugar in return and as she asked the sasquatch, had heard the girls friend and pulled a hair off of himself and traded the girl for the sugar.

For me I don't need to hear those things I've seen two of these things up close and they are all not the same. Some are laid back and some are mean. I had one scare me off the mountain but didn't chase me and I had one that threw rocks at me and my sister on the way home from school one spring day. I know what's out there I don't need no proof I've been through a whole mess of incidents and I just add 2 and 2 together and I got my answer my whole life was a buildup to prepare me for the next phase but it was going to be way different than what most others go through.

We all go through phases but I guess for me being born an identical twin born with extra everything I felt when the lord took my brother he placed all of who he was in my soul as well. I mean I can feel out a situation. I can pick the good from the bad in people. I can pick out the good athletes in a pickup game. I dream stuff that happens down the road and I experience it again, just a lot of extra little gifts.

I honestly feel like that's why when I go into the woods if there is one of these wicked beautiful creatures somewhere close or near he or she or they will come and feel me out. It's happened more than once. Shit it's happened more than 3 times, those were just the good ones. Gotta laugh about that one there wow but true.

One day I just woke up and decided finally to go for it push for the truth. Put my pieces of the puzzle in the pot and let's all start putting the puzzle together. I knew what I had experienced would light a fire out there under people's asses and get them up off the couch and out into the woods instead of inside not living. I spent half of my life in the woods and I loved it but my health limits me these days. But hell I already know a ton compared to most others.

Why 20 years, that's why you name it. I've done it out in the forest. Started very young, that was my turn key for me. It was my safe haven for a long time. Now I just work with all my people that are pushing for the truth, there are many people let me tell you. This has become a big topic lately.

All this started with great people who told me just let it go and you will feel so much better. I think It was right there in that moment I became free from it, finally letting it all out there. Starting with Sasquatch theory, Leslie G over at Cryptids Canada she's become a good friend. We are still working my encounter stories, see you forget the little things then when you clean house little things come out that may be important so you tell them too, always.

I then got with Sasquatch Odyssey,did an interview. Started to feel good about it. Next I met up with so many others who were working hard. I want to tell you who's working hard out there my dude (Steve how to hunt) he really made me comfortable the more I watched him go I'd go as well. Push even more.
Les and his work,Todd and his work,my buddy Chris over at Bigfoot Real Encounters. Buckeye Bigfoot, the R.M.S.O. and others as well.

So many really pushing, that's not all of them that is a drop in the bucket. My buddy Todd Earys over at Cryptids podcast we interviewed Sunday the 25th of April. It took a lot of work to get the show done but we got it complete. I've done all my work and research and even all my writing for my books has been done by this Moto G. I've put it through hell let's say that I have to say Todd taught me a lot to watching his shows with les.

Then I met Albert Ledesma (Albie) A Buddhist and a Shaman, A pure soul just as myself. We met and it was like pancakes and syrup. He taught me so much about Sasquatch and fast. All of what I didn't know and how they had probably been drawn to me from my first time in the woods. And after he educated me and after I watched his videos 1-4, I knew that he was right. I had no clue ,well some clue, but I was young and naive. I know now it just makes me feel better to know I had a hunch after letting all my encounters out to the world it had been a lifelong pattern.

So grateful to have met him and the knowledge he gave me was (PRICELESS) everyone who is new to this subject just watch his work he makes it easy even for the new and uneducated. There's so much information out there about these creatures. It will exhaust you day after day trying to soak it all up like a sponge as I have. It has me worn out to the maximum so after I complete this book I will take a break for a couple days. I have 2 books at publish now being reviewed we are hoping to get published if not I will be patient they will eventually get published it's all about patience in this world.

I have the first book Blessed and Cursed to publish as well as a company Voyage media working with me on a possible movie pitch about the manuscript I sent them about this new tell all. As well as Bigfoot And Steller Jay has been sent to many publishers. It is a kids book to help educate them a little bit about bigfoot so they have the basics when they go into the woods.

I'm so glad I did this, I feel so relieved now that it is off my chest. I'm a new man that is for sure. I have researched and met new people in the field, worked written 24/7/7 days a week since this all started for about 3 months now, it is tiring work but even if it doesn't pay, it still pays off for me. Maybe one day my book will become a movie. After all it is a tell all so much knowledge of how they move ,how they work, how they mimic us, how they take to survive but also will return items.

How they can almost read our damn minds. How they migrate from high up to the valley floors,following the game,very powerful yet intelligent creature/animal/hominid/hybrid-hominid. So many opinions have been given by great PHD's many on there makeup how did they originate,how long have they been here.

Were all still learning but making great progress as we all move forward together trying to get new organizations going and teaming up with others to push even further. If we could get a grant for Research equipment that would be great but very hard to achieve. There are organizations already out there making big moves with their own money to push towards the truth.

See that's what makes it bitter sweet for me. I already know the truth. Seeing one at just 8 years old, only to see one again at 25 years of age but close up at 40 feet and having a whole scary situation with it as well jumping off of the side of a mountain and rolling all the way down because fear kept me from using my damn legs. So scary but so much energy coming from that experience.

I only hope that we can really make a good solid run this spring and this year towards learning some more key information. We already know they are trying to communicate with others they are gifting, they are clearly making huge structures for us to see. A warning to not truck any further or to show off or a bit of both.

Some of the tree breaks are so impressive and some trees being flipped upside down and stuck in top first, really impressive.

Now that's showing off. They are starting to really interact in some ways. Yet they still maintain that perfection when it comes to being evasive and defensive. They move in such ways that blow the average mind. I've seen it. They are fast. They toy with you, get in your mind, they make you think but on impulse you make your choices on what to do next that's how we all make the crucial errors in video recording and trying to get pictures of them.

Throw all that out, you just go with the basics in my opinion. A regular 5 snapshot from Kroger, maybe grab 3 just in case, go to a hotspot or a spot where you have had hot action. Early in the day is a good time. My encounter was between 3-4 am, coming down for a drink of water I caught him with his hand in the drink. Early dusk is good depending on the season, dress in camo, doe urine to de-scent yourself. Just after dark I've learned is good as well from research, so dusk,right after sunset,or shortly before 3-6 am.

They always hold the high ground remember that one. But they eventually travel down to drink and eat and do their thing. They are nocturnal, they can see very well and hear very well and smell very well. Like most animals they will migrate the same trail unless threatened. They are very fast, and have a huge arm span and gate as they travel 4-6 feet each step. They cover ground quickly, if you encounter one you never make eye contact, look down or away.

Hold your composure and walk away slowly but as normal as possible. Don't talk or try to communicate unless they do. There are different clans, different breeds, different attitudes, so you never know what the situation will be that's why I say only go on the hunt if your really keen on what it is your after because they always stay one if not two up on us every move,every thought every action and reaction as well. Its called tools for survival and they have them all and then some.

These Creatures are built for speed you will not outrun one, you will get caught ran down. Their powerful as anything I've ever seen. Strength that's out of this world. I don't believe they are from another planet I don't believe they cloak, I believe they have been here since before the Indians and they should be able to claim rights to the woods. I also believe we should leave them alone.

In this book, I've told my True Encounter stories.

As well as tried to educate on how life can go after having a full

on encounter. It didn't go to well for myself but my life was going

to be different from the moment I was born. I knew it after I was

old enough to know I was an identical twin. Shortly after I started

to experience crazy things in life.

I've seen some things others wouldn't want to see or maybe

would but I have to say are you really willing to go through the

hell and torment with your soul after you get a sighting. So many

emotions consume you slowly, engulf you and I'm just lucky that I

got the chance to walk out of it all still alive. That's being totally

honest. I've been hospitalized so many times clinging to life from

not being able to handle what I'd seen and gone through over

the years after the fact. So to the ones out there looking, you

need to read this before you get serious. I'm being totally

serious.

It is no joke once your stuck in the point of no return and your

right smack in the middle of the woods maybe unarmed, no bear

mace ,don't even know if that would work. You are just flat out

screwed and one is closeup on you. Somehow someway it's

happened and now your where you never thought you would be

in the heat of the moment, 500-1000 creatures closeup on you.

Your frozen with fear. It knows you are. It already knows if you are a pure soul or if your an evil soul or if it already knows what you are do you.

I would just say really think about it before you make the move because the forest in all its beauty will still swallow you up never to return. So go extra prepared, you adjust by the days you'll be there as well as the weather. It can change at the drop of a hat. Always prepare and plot your location and tell others when your returning.

The hotspots updated, Pennsylvania jumped to #3 Recently. Washington,Oregon,Ohio #4, Alaska, Canada and Florida, Georgia,California #1, Alabama. There has been a lot of action in these places lately, even great video clips as well as reports of missing people. Again, always safety first. Plot a safety plan and double check your grid and location. So if someone does go missing the search teams will have a better layout to search from.

It's become a dangerous game of cat and mouse out there, usually the clans of the National forest are known to just be playful, not violent with people. But at times have been known to freak and scare people from their campsites. It's the smaller clans you need to worry about and the loners. They may not be as nice. So in different areas people have to be extra cautious we are sharing the woods now and it's becoming so much more clear now.

We have to learn to respect them as they do us and not try to harm them or shoot them, they are and have been mostly peaceful unless provoked. If miss treated as anything on earth is known to try to defend itself. So it's all about peace and tranquility when we walk into the forests and woods across the United States, because once what was hardly seen is now being seen constantly.

That is a total game changer and many people won't even notice the change. We have to learn to live with one another, times have become so crazy since the epidemic started. People are not the same in their minds and it won't go unnoticed trust that. So reach out for help instead of diving in the depths like I did after having to suppress my full on encounter on Toms Mountain. I allowed the situation to take me almost all the way out, almost ending my life.

Before you can't turn back, it is not all fun and games out there and some don't understand that until it's to late,as I did. It became a struggle within the forces of my soul and I didn't even see it coming. It hit me like a ton of bricks and I was consumed before I even knew what was going on.

I'm just grateful and blessed to still be alive and on this beautiful green earth, to be able to enjoy the woods again. I hope now that I let all of this out to the world, I can walk once again into the forest and be at peace once again with the forest again,and be able to enjoy all the extras in life it gives me. It will all come back to me. I never forgot how much I loved fishing and hiking until I wrote this book.

I am even planning a trip out to Todds Creek in Morrow Ohio with a good friend of mine, Tim Ragle. And go to where I had my 2nd encounter with Chris Garrett. We plan to fish this time without being ran out of the woods, if something happens there will be a Todds Creek part 2 I guess. The trip is planned for may 2nd 2021. I will be taking an audio device as well as a couple instant cameras just in case, after all I'm still researching for more material to write about. I have Completed (Bigfoot And Stellar Jay) April 19th 2021.It is at the publisher this is my 2nd book and when this is complete, my 3rd and 4th will soon follow.
At some point I may travel out to Miami White Water Forest and Camp and do research for a couple days, sasquatch seem to be

all in my realm wherever I end up in the woods they end up close to me at some point off and on why I will probably never know but to have 2 full sightings and encounters in my life with other countless incidents of rock throwing as well as sounds in the night.

As well as a few times during foul weather while out in the deep woods of Ohio, Kentucky, Indiana,I can say without a doubt in my mind they exist, how? Why? I've seen them up close not once but twice, as well as my uncle Doug Hogan and his story of seeing a breed of sasquatch in the forests of Cambodia while at war in Vietnam, just a smaller version of them he'd said but still a very impressive creature especially at night time they were so fast and efficient with every move.

To many things happened but in a perfect sequence for me to learn about these creatures I just wasn't paying attention until I was put right up on one. There is nothing more frightful in life I promise you to see a sasquatch up close. The feeling one gets is pure rush of adrenaline followed by being mortally paralyzed by fear. As your frozen, your mind is speeding at a million miles an hour. What is that I'm looking at, they said they didn't exist they, said they were a myth.

It feels as if your in a Hollywood movie scene somehow, someway being filmed and you weren't informed. There are so many emotions, so many questions, zooming through your mind. But in split seconds your processing it all then your realize it's real life and your able to break away from being hypnotized, no better way to explain it and you flee out of you're fear. In my case I lost total use of my legs for 5 minutes, struggling to get use of them to get down off of Toms Mountain.

My future plans may be to take a crew back out towards Toms Mountain,once I finish both books, it may be on the table to make a go of it, depending on a couple situations I have going on with my life right now. I should have kept the writing of my books secret and not tried to build them up so damn much. I really pushed hard setting up interviews and having videos of my encounters on YouTube. I thought doing it this way would really help the buildup and also writing all of my books in a backward sequence to keep the excitement to a maximum.

Last but not least we took a trip down to Kentucky in June of 20201, my last expedition as my health was declining I knew this would be the last trip for me. My buddy Rim Ragle and I went down to Whitley county Kentucky and visited his father and mother right off of the bat we found a set of deer legs on the back of the property down next to the pond on their land. This was before we even set out anywhere. They looked like they had been twisted off of a deer.

The second day we broke out the boat and went to fish the morrow river. We were at the boat dock and backing the boat in, there was a ridge above us, I was by myself as John Ragle was backing the boat in and Tim Ragle was sitting in the boat. Driving it in the water i was guiding John when from up off of the ridge something was thrown at me. I looked to see if I could find a trace of what had been thrown, I couldn't find anything.

We got the boat in the water and we were off to fish. About an hour, later off in the woods behind us ,we heard a huge tree get pushed over and it landed like a missile. So loud it rattled our ears as we jumped in the air off of the boat. We knew that it really got weird and I wondering what we had in the area with us, it would all pay off later.

We were in a cove a couple of hours later when I was taking pictures of the woods when a gust of wind came through and boom a storm started to wipe us out on the boat. No cover, we drove back to the dock getting lost a couple of times but finally made it. The next day we said our goodbyes and we were on our way after having a good expedition and a couple good pieces of evidence. Tim was finally talking about Sasquatch himself.

When we rolled through a town called Berea Kentucky, I look over to my right as I was sight seeing and looking for evidence, once again, I look up and at about 2000 feet I see a tree deforest situation happening up top of a mountain. They had cleared a huge portion of the top out, not a tree one but on high ground I though a little bit weird to me.

But as I look down and off to the left I start to see tree breaks at about 8 feet high. At this point Tim is already looking and stifled by what he's seeing. Wow, he says wow,now that's wild now I'm a believer he says. After all these years of being on the neutral line I do believe now. I told him see what I've been saying all along. Tim brother, there is just times when you find evidence that is so so and there are times you find evidence that'll just blow you away.

And this trip was one of em we had found not one but four key pieces of evidence in just only two days time. A very good short expedition in my opinion. I'd seen plenty, I knew what was happening the Sasquatch were clearly upset that there high ground had been taken from them.

The End

Written by Jeffrey David Lilly Jr.

Blessed and Cursed

True Encounter Stories

by

Jeffrey David Lilly Jr

Dedications

Jeff And Dorothy Lilly my mother and father.

I am also dedicating this book to my brother Jason Michael Lilly.

He went with the Lord November 10th,2020. We miss you dearly.

And to Angela Michele Skeens who told me - "Let it go, get it off

of your conscience and share what you know with the world."

Author Bio

Jeffrey David Lilly Jr has spent more than 20 years in the field of bigfoot study. He has logged countless hours reviewing alleged bigfoot videos as well as talking to numerous first hand account witnesses. Jeffrey also enjoys taking time to fishing, hunting and to go camping. He currently resides in Ohio.

Look for these other great titles from Zombie Media

Bigfoot and Steller Jay's River Day

The Leaf Lady at the Amber Estates

True Short Stories of the Paranormal: My Personal Experiences

The Adventures of Pete Johnson and the Ghosts of Scott's Mountain

Understanding Bigfoot

Bigfoot Witness

My Haunted House and other Weird Tales

I saw a UFO: Mysteries of the sky

Bigfoot and Eastern Cousins

Sasquatch Family Ties

The Ivory-billed Woodpecker:Taunting Extinction

Available on Amazon and other fine retailers